I0477442

HOME & OFFICE SECURITY

Protection of Residences & Businesses

Orlando "Andy" Wilson

Orlando "Andy" Wilson

CONTENTS

RESIDENTIAL & OFFICE SECURITY

The security of your home is a main priority but when most people think about this, they are only considering the threats from thieves or burglars. Well, there are quite a few other things that you need to consider especially if you're an investigator or political journalist.

One of the biggest security threats are the people you let into your residence. You should all be aware that if someone you don't know turns up at your front door you should not let them in, even if they claim to be from a utilities company etc. If they don't have an appointment don't open the door and turn them away. If they are persistent then call the police... If someone claiming to be a police officer turns up unexpectedly at your door always verify their identity with their dispatch or station, real cops will understand your concerns!

That young and respectable looking woman knocking on your door could be there to check if anyone is home, to look at your security procedures, if you let her in, she will see the layout of your house and if you have anything worth stealing or she could be trying to plant a listening device. Think about your procedures for answering the door to a stranger, and ensure your children understand never to open the door to a stranger.

I have had clients who attended my courses and when I asked them how well they knew the cleaners and gardeners they hired the answer was they had no clue who they were. Most seemed to hire from an agency, or they were sent by a company. Generally, that's fine if the agency or company are vetting their staff properly or, better still, know them personally but many don't.

The domestic help industry is all about hard work, but generally its very poorly paid. So, it tends to attract those new to a country, or those that may have problems obtaining work papers. I am in no way saying that these people are bad, quite the opposite, many times they are dependent on the job and will not do anything stupid to jeopardize it. What I am saying is always check to make sure that if they come from a 3rd party they are known and trusted. It's best to always do things by recommendation and check references.

The potential issue that comes to most people's minds when letting someone into their home is that they can steal things, which is the obvious one. There is also the issue of people committing illegal activity such as drug use etc. which I will talk about a little later. One potential problem that many ignore is letting visitors use their Wi-Fi and freely giving out passwords. Do you know what these people are searching the web for? If it's child pornography you're going to have a problem. If they are running an internet scam, threatening or blackmailing people all this will come back to your IP address. My advice would be to try to use parental blocks on your Wi-Fi and change the passwords regularly.

Most people have friends over to visit, many have dinner parties etc. My question is how well do you know your guests? People in general are nosy, and many will want to wander through your house, with or without permission. If you don't want people to wander around then lock doors and try to block hallways, pet or child gates attached to an alarm can be a good and affordable deterrent.

The other issue arising from living with others, in general, is people being let into your home without your knowledge. A live-in nanny can sneak her boyfriend in, just as your teenage daughter can. I will touch on an issue here that mainly concerns firearms.

I had a client come through my classes who had grown up in a Latin American country where his family owned a farm. One night his father heard a noise in the house, grabbed his legally owned pistol and went to investigate. When he walked in the kitchen, he bumped into a man in boxer shorts and shot him thinking he was an intruder. In reality, the man was the boyfriend of one of the live-in staff and had gone to the kitchen to get something to drink; he was also a police officer. In many places this would have been regarded as a justifiable shooting, a genuine mistake but, the country was going communist, landowners were not in a favorable position and the police were not happy one of their own was shot... The father, the shooter, was sentenced to prison on a murder charge. He later died in prison...

Every now and again in the US there is a case where one family member shoots another, due to mistaking them for an intruder in their homes. If firearms are kept for home security, there must always be good communication between family members as to who is staying in the house and when people are coming and going. There is no room for mistakes, and you can't be overcautious.

Residential & Office Security - The Basics

Residential security (RS) is something that is usually taken very lightly, most believe putting in an alarm system and maybe a camera or two is all that's required. It is common knowledge that one of the favored places for criminals and terrorists to target a victim is when they are in, entering or leaving their residence; RS must be taken very seriously. In times of civil unrest looters will be looking to target any location that has valuables, weapons or assets that they can use and that has minimal security, this means most residential properties.

If your threat is from criminals or terrorists and you're going to hire security personnel for your residence or office make sure they are in some way trustworthy, just because someone has a security or private investigators license it does not mean they are competent or not working with the criminals. What a lot of people forget when hiring security personnel is that you get what you pay for. I am approached all the time by people who require security personnel, many of whom are having problems with their current security contractor, but they do not want to pay a professional rate. Sure, you can always get a cheaper option but don't expect the budget security guard to be too concerned about your assets or wellbeing.

The basic procedures I have listed here can be applied on all residences or offices. What will differ is the type and size of the residence, the manpower and budget available. When taking over or moving into a residence, a threat assessment must be compiled, and all vulnerable spots identified. A set of orders needs to be compile, and procedures drawn up for every eventuality. Before you occupy a residence, the residence and its grounds need to be searched for IEDs, electronic surveillance devices and contraband such as illegal drugs or weapons that could have been left there by the previous occupants.

If the budget allows, electronic security devices should be employed. There is a vast array of security devices available on the commercial market, ranging from CCTV to laser sensors. Always choose the best that you can afford and buy it from a reputable dealer; it is best to also get a service agreement and have all equipment regularly serviced by trusted people. Even if your residence is in an apartment block, CCTV should be considered for the corridors and public parts of the building. Covert and portable CCTV systems are available at affordable prices and have a variety of uses. These days there are also affordable CCTV systems that you can monitor over the internet. I had one client who told me while he was working in East Africa, he watched Hurricane Katrina destroy his house in Louisiana over the internet. Remember if you use internet camera's they can be hacked into, if someone gets access to your computers, passwords or on a more professional level access to your server they can also see what you're up to.

Many people have alarms systems and panic buttons in their residences, and it amuses me that a lot of people believe that installing an alarm is all they require to protect their families. We have all seen the adverts on TV where a woman is home alone, the alarm goes off, the bad guy runs away, and the alarm company phones her to make sure she is OK. If only the world was that perfect. What if the bad guys aren't worried and expect an alarm to go off because they know they have at least 15 minutes before the police will respond? If you have an alarm system then you need to know what the response time will be for those responding, be it an armed response company or the local police. In some places the response can take hours, even in the US. If the responding police believe there is a serious incident taking place, with shots fired, they will usually back off, call for support, cordon the area and assemble a SWAT team to respond. If you're lucky this may take an hour or two!

Another criminal tactic to counter an alarm system on a residence is to keep setting them off until the target turns the system off. Think about it, if over a period of two weeks the alarm on your back door keeps going off between 1am to 4am what would you do? Initially for the first few alarm activations the police will respond, in a lot of places after 3 false alarm activations the police will no longer respond. If you have an armed response company, they will be charging you for every alarm they respond to. So, I am sure you will call out the alarm company to fix the alarm, but they will find nothing wrong with it. Would you keep putting up with the cost and aggravation of the apparently false alarm activations or just turn the alarm off? Take nothing at face value, if you have an alarm that starts going off for no apparent reason, look deeper!

Security for a residence needs to be planned in depth with multiple rings of defense, how many you have will depend on the type and size of the residence. When planning the security for a residence you need to think like the criminals. In 1994 I was working in South Africa and was tasked to provide security for numerous residences that had active threats on them. My working day usually started in the early evening and went through to after first light the next morning. When I arrived at a residence the first thing I would do would be to assess the area around the residence for likely criminal surveillance points and approach routes. I would then assess the fence or wall around the garden for the most likely point that the criminals would use for entry. I would then take up a position in the garden where I could see the likely criminal entry point or points and as much of the residence as possible, then I waited.

So, the first cordon of security you should consider is the general area around the residence. You need to identify any potential surveillance positions, choke points and possible ambush locations. Consider using CCTV to cover the streets and exterior of the walls of your grounds. All routes leading up to the residence need to be regularly searched for IEDs, surveillance and signs of an ambush which may be in the process of being set up, to do this the routes and exterior would need to be walked by trusted and alert personnel.

If your residence is in an apartment block, then the next level of security could take the form of covert CCTV in public areas or placing the building under general protective surveillance. In a large house, this cordon will be the walls or hedges that surround the grounds; these can be monitored by CCTV, with sensors or where legal be topped with razor or electric wire.

In a large residence the next cordon would be the grounds or garden. This area could be covered by CCTV and be patrolled regularly by security personnel, day and night and in all weather. All external buildings such as garages and tool sheds need to be properly secured.

A lot of people ask me about using guard dogs, something which I tend to dissuade people from doing. Dogs can be weapons and must be kept under control. While working in South Africa I had two German Sheppard's attack me; they did not die because the client was screaming at me not to shoot them. The dogs had been let out of their cage, as they usually were in the evening, by a staff member who did not know that I was working there. OK, it was only me, so no problems, but what if it was a child or woman, and the dog's owner was not there to take control of them?

If you use dogs they must be properly trained, if I was in a high-risk area would I consider having trained dogs in my garden, sure but they would need to be properly trained. Dogs can be targeted as same as security personnel, if they are not trained properly, they are easy to poison. Guard dogs that bark a lot are easy to counter, same as an alarm system. We have used this tactic numerous times in parts of Latin America where every house seems to have a pack of dogs, you just need to get the dogs barking and keep them barking. Then in a short time the owner will soon get fed up with the noise, or the dogs will get tired.

The next cordon would be the residence itself, all doors, windows and skylights need to be secured and controlled and if possible, alarmed. Consider defensive gardening to deter criminals gaining access to windows; below the windows plant thorny bushes that would make it difficult and noisy for the criminals to get through. Ideally, all rooms should be fitted with motion detectors and in high-risk areas locked when not in use.

Now you need to consider what you are going to do if criminals try to make entry to your residence; you need to make plans and preparations for this. On my courses I usually ask people what they would have done if someone tried to break into their house the previous night? A lot of people say they don't know or just then start to think about it. You need to put together sensible procedures, and then if you have a break in, you will know what to do and not panic.

There are two general considerations when planning your procedures; are you going to stay in the residence or evacuate, what you do will depend on your situation. A secure room needs to be designated within the residence to be used as a safe room for you and your family in the event of an attack where immediate evacuation is not practical.

The room should be lockable from the inside and have several good communications links with the outside world; there should be a list of emergency numbers in the room, so help can be summoned in the event of an emergency. What equipment is in the room will depend on your situation and the length of time you will need to possibly stay in the room. This is where you need to know the approximate response times of those coming to help you. The main thing a safe room needs is an escape route. If I was a criminal and wanted to target someone who I knew took their security serious I would not enter their residence. If someone knows how to defend a building, then SWAT and room clearing tactics won't work. The easiest way to clear a building is to cordon it off, and set it on fire, then shoot or abduct the inhabitants as they exit. And, if they don't exit then the criminals have saved some bullets. So, always have an escape route!

A set of procedures will need to be drawn up for dealing with visitors to the residence; this is the downfall of most residential security programs. A good example of this resulted in the kidnapping in Haiti of a family member of a business associate of mine. This person has a large residence and employed an armed guard to man his front gate. One evening the guard opened the gate to talk with someone who was asking after one of the staff members, as soon as he stepped outside the gate, he had a gun to put to his head by a criminal who was waiting next to the gate. The criminal with their crew gained access to the main residence, as the doors were left unlocked, they then robbed the place and kidnapped four people.

Why should the criminals try to break into a residence when in a lot of cases they can get the occupants to easily open the doors and come to them? As you read this now what would you do if someone crashed into your car outside your house or office? You would go outside and see what had happened right? Now you can be kidnapped, and the bad guys have access to your house or business. A lot of houses have their electric mains outside, same in places where generators are used. So, if the criminals cut the power what will most people do? Go out and investigate! Cut the connecting cables to most people satellite TV and what will they do? Go outside and check the dish? So, why break into a house when it is very easy to get people to come outside and bypass all their security procedures for you!

Residential Security Checklist

Here is a list of things you want to consider when planning the security for your residence. Not everything will apply to you but take what does and use it, a lot of the considerations here can be applied to most houses, apartments or offices etc.

• Always plan security in depth, you want as many cordons of defense as possible.

• Have several means of communications; landlines and cellular and check them regularly.

• Have planned escape routes.

• If the residence is overlooked, what sniper or surveillance positions are there?

• Check to see if the residence is under surveillance?

• Has the residence been searched for IEDs, electronic surveillance devices or contraband?

• Is the residence ever left unoccupied, if yes, then it needs to be searched before re-occupation?

• Does the residence have a fence or wall around it, and can it realistically keep out intruders?

• Are there gates to the residence, can they stop an intruder or a car, are the gates always locked and what are the procedures for greeting visitors?

• Is there anything to help criminals climb over the garden walls or gates, such as trees or poles around the exterior of the property?

• If the residence is in an apartment block, are there fire escapes or scaffolding that could give the criminals a way in?

• Where along the routes in and out of the residence could an ambush be concealed?

• Consider putting the residence under protective surveillance.

• Always use counter-surveillance drills before entering and upon exiting the residence.

• Regularly photograph or video the areas surrounding the residence and always watch for suspicious vehicles and people.

• What security lights are there, do they work, when are the lights turned on and where is their control switch? If the control switch is outside, move it inside.

• Lights should shine away from the residence not on to it.

• Consider attaching lights triggered by movement detectors outside of doors and vulnerable areas.

• Any defects to floodlighting or other security lights should be fixed ASAP.

• If you are in an apartment block, is the reception manned 24hrs a day and if yes, are the people manning it competent? Consider a penetration test.

• Do your doors have peepholes. If yes, peepholes are best positioned at the side of the door or in the wall. So, for example you cannot be shot through the door when looking through the peephole. If using a peephole always extinguish any lights so your shadow can not be seen from the outside.

• Consider using a video phone to greet visitors and CCTV cameras to cover the doors and surrounding areas.

• Consider an armored layer on the inside of main doors.

• If you have a residential security team (RST) do they know their orders?

• Are the RST from a quality and trustworthy company and have they been vetted and well trained?

• Do an assessment on your security personnel and evaluate how much you can really trust them; will they fight, flee or just rollover if there is a problem.

• Make sure the RST always patrols the grounds and in all weathers; bad weather is the best time for attacks as guards are usually seeking shelter and un-alert.

• If you are using guard dogs, make sure that they are well trained and preferably under the control of their handler.

• Are all doors to the residence solid and are the doorframes solid? Most times a doorframe will break before the lock on the door.

• Are the locks on the doors of a good quality and have you changed them since taking over the residence?

• If a key is lost or an employee is fired who has access to keys, then change your locks.

• Consider using deadbolts at the top and bottom of a door and, also wedges in conjunction with the normal locks.

• Can the locks be unlocked from the outside if a window is broken, or can the door hinges be unscrewed?

• Do you have control of all the keys to the residence and have a list of everyone that has keys?

• Have all unused entrances and exits been secured?

• All windows need to be secured on all floors of the building. It is a fact that in 90% of burglaries, access is gained through windows. Check that all windows are properly shut, secured and if possible alarmed.

• Consider putting thorny bushes under windows and around the perimeter of your garden to deter intruders. Thorny bushes can be put on the inside of perimeter walls to tangle up and alert you to anyone jumping over.

• Use laminated glass and heavy curtains where there is a threat from IEDs as they will help prevent flying glass. Wood blinds also work for extra privacy and protection.

• Beware of casting shadows against windows which can be seen from the outside.

• Consider putting a gravel walkway around the outside of your house so you can hear anyone approaching or stalking around.

• All skylights and roof doors need to be secured and preferably alarmed. Roofs need to be secured and monitored.

• Is the attic of the residence adjoined to another roof or attic, from which someone could gain access?

• What alarms are in the residence, are they working and when were they last tested?

• All doors and windows on outbuildings need to be secured, regularly checked and, if possible, alarmed.

• Are the roofs of the outbuildings secured? An IED or assailant on the roof of a garage stands a better chance of not being spotted than one in a driveway.

• Do all padlocks have spare keys and who has them?

• Are the padlocks of good quality and difficult to pick or shim?

• Are all weapons in the residence legal and are they secured when not in use?

• Do you and the RST know their rules of engagement and the laws for use of force?

• No vehicle should be given access to the grounds of the residence without a member of the security team at least physically checking the interior of the passenger compartment. You never know, your personal driver who is flashing his lights and laying on his horn at the front gate in the early hours of the morning, might have a gun pointed at the back of this head or a bomb in the trunk of his car.

• What firefighting equipment is there in the residence and is it in a serviceable condition?

• Are there any fire alarms and do they work? Fire is the largest cause of loss and damage to private and commercial properties. Fire prevention is, therefore, one of the highest residential security concerns.

• Flooding is a major threat to property and equipment, common causes include taps that have been left running, leaks in plumbing systems or faulty air conditioning systems, heavy rain or snowfall.

• Are all valuables kept secure, and do you have pictures of all valuable artwork and jewelry etc.?

• Are all valuables insured, and have you recorded the serial numbers of all TVs, computers and all valuable equipment?

• Do you and your family, and staff have security and emergency procedures in place? And does everyone know them?

• Do you and your family, and staff know how to report any suspicious activity?

• Do you and your family, and staff know how to raise the alarm, in the case of an emergency?

• Make arrangements for power cuts, keep spare batteries and bulbs for flashlights, with several means of communications and check them regularly.

• If you have a backup generator, ensure it is serviceable, and you have plenty of fuel in a secure location.

• Keep all sensitive and security documentation secure and confidential.

• Keep computers and hard drives secure and password protected.

• Ensure your internet connections, internal and external phone and data cables are secure and not hackable.

• Have your staff and employees been profiled and had background checks?

• Do not discuss sensitive or security related subjects in front of staff, consider giving them disinformation on such things as travel and business plans.

• Don't let any of the security personnel get over familiar with any of the other staff.

• Consider monitoring all phone calls from, and into the residence.

• All contractors must have appointments and must be searched before entering and leaving the residence. Searched when entering to check for contraband, IEDs or electronic surveillance devices, and when leaving to make sure they are not stealing anything.

• Contractors should be accompanied at all times.

• If suspicious of visitors, then turn them away or keep them outside and preferably illuminated, until their credentials are verified. Also consider that they could be testing your security or a distraction while others try to access your residence.

• Never illuminate yourself in a doorway or a window, darkness is your friend.

• All deliveries should go through the RST and be checked for anything suspicious and have a secure area to isolate any suspicious packages.

• Use a mailbox or virtual office address rather than your residential address.

• Be suspicious of unexpected power outages or faulty alarms etc.

• Always have escape routes and don't let security procedures obstruct them.

• Know the location and safest routes to safe houses, emergency rendezvous points, and hospitals, etc.

• Think like a criminal and plan for every eventuality.

SECURITY CONSIDERATIONS FOR REALTORS

Any type of meeting can be extremely dangerous and should always be treated with caution, this is where people will know where you will be at a specific time. This is just what the bad guys want to know! Arranging meetings is an easy way to set someone up for kidnapping, assassination, sexual assault or robbery.

I spoke with Jerry Arrechea a corporate security manager and world champion martial artist based in Mexico City. Mexico has one of the highest crime rates in the world, so I wanted to know what Jerry recommends to his clients for keeping themselves safe.

In Mexico we must deal with a wide array of security problems ranging from drug cartel violence to general street crime and there is no magic solution. The criminals here are professional; they plan and organize their crimes from the initial surveillance of their targets to how to escape after the crimes have been committed. It's important for us to be able to identify the criminals in the surveillance and planning stage of their operations and to take counter measures. The last thing we want is a confrontation as the criminals are usually very well armed and not afraid to shoot, we would sooner lose goods or money than put our clients in hostile situations.

One situation where we are always extra careful is when we are attending meetings in unfamiliar areas especially with people, who we don't know 100% as these meetings could be set ups for robberies or kidnappings. Before the meeting we do a thorough due diligence check on those we are meeting with, and on the day of the meeting we sweep the area looking for anyone or any vehicles that look suspicious. We usually employ protective surveillance personnel while the meeting is taking place to alert us of any suspicious activity that may take place in the area.

I advise all my clients, especially females to be cautious when attending meetings where they will be isolated, even if they are meeting with people they know to some degree. I have a female self-defense client who is a luxury real estate agent and has had several issues with clients over the years, who have tried to sexually assault her while she is showing properties. These days she always has a male driver take her to the appointments and has worked out a plan of action if she is attacked. She also always has something close at hand that she can use as a weapon. The last wannabe playboy, someone who she had met before, that tried to touch her inappropriately, ended up with two broken fingers and a broken nose. All her driver had to do when he came to her assistance was to throw the now whimpering playboy off the property....

This lady's driver is a well-trained and dedicated guy, but it still took him time after being alerted to get to her location. She feels it can be intimidating for her clients if she had a bodyguard shadowing her, so her driver usually waits in the car. This is why she had worked out her immediate reaction drill as she knew it would take 15 to 45 seconds for her driver to get to her assistance. Everyone should think about how they would react to an assault and put a plan in place. Even if you are in an area where the police will come quickly to your assistance, you must know how to alert them that you're in danger and then protect yourself until they are able to get to you. As I said earlier, there is no magic fix, you must be aware of your environment and have plans in place for how to avoid potentially hostile situations and in the worst-case scenarios how to use force to defend yourself!

DUTIES OF A RESIDENTIAL SECURITY TEAM (RST)

The downfall of most RSTs is poor management. After a while team members start to get complacent either through boredom or low morale. On long term jobs RST members should not be allowed or forced to work endless amounts of shifts. Even if the team member wants to, they should not really work more than six days in a row. Everyone needs time off to catch up on sleep and sort out personal administration. The management should regularly visit the residence and speak to the RST/BGs and find out if there are any problems, update procedures and speak to the client. If a team member is letting the team down by sleeping on duty, turning up for duty late or being incompetent, they must be dismissed; if not, they could bring down the morale of the other team members.

Duties To Be Undertaken

• Residential security duties including control of access and egress.

• Checking and completion of documentation, passes or permits.

• Search of vehicles, areas, baggage and persons where authorized.

• Escort of persons, goods, baggage or vehicles.

• Vehicle marshalling and control.

• Arrest and detention of persons where authorized.

• Investigation and reporting of crime and/or incidents.

• Taking and recording statements.

• Foot patrols.

• Safety and fire prevention patrols and inspections.

• Inspections of safety and fire prevention equipment.

• Operation of security equipment.

• Liaison with Statutory Authorities as necessary.

• Completion of logs, reports and safety records.

• Dealing with emergencies such as firefighting where equipped and authorized, supervising evacuation drills, bomb or IED searches and administrating first aid.

Patrol Duties

In this section you will learn about the concept of patrolling. It is important to remember that the contents of each subsection that follows will be affected to some extent by the client that you work for. Each client is different, and patrolling duties will vary from one assignment to another. It must be stressed that patrols can identify and prevent minor problems from becoming major disasters, as long as the patrolling guards are alert and thorough.

Whilst patrolling an assignment your objectives should be:

• To prevent and detect theft and other offenses against the customer's interest.

• To prevent and detect fire.

• To prevent and detect flood and other types of damage.

• To ensure that the client's rules are not broken.

• To prevent accidents.

To patrol in a professional manner, you must be aware of what to look for. The first part of this section will tell you about the principal security hazards.

Security Hazards

On most residential assignments there will be specific areas, such as offices or buildings that should be always locked for security purposes. If there are any signs of interference with the doors, windows or locks in these areas, you should take immediate action as detailed in the Assignment Instructions.

• It is a fact that in 90% of cases involving burglary, access to premises is gained through windows. Check that windows are shut and secured. If it appears that a member of staff has forgotten to lock a secure area, secure it yourself (if you can), make a note of it in your notebook and inform your control room/office.

• When patrolling the perimeter, check for defects in the fencing or walls surrounding the premises. A new gap in a fence should be secured as best as possible and the same reporting procedures carried out.

• Check outbuildings for signs of interference.

• Any defects to floodlighting or other security lights should be reported to your control room/office and the customer informed as soon as possible.

• Always be alert for flashlights or other lighting that is not normally present, as this may indicate intruders.

• Challenge and investigate any strangers that you meet in the course of your patrol. Do so politely, as they may be genuine visitors.

• If vehicles are parked on the premises, then check that they are secure and that ignition keys have been removed (if this is the policy on site).

• If checking of vehicles is involved as part of your duties, then pay special attention to areas where visiting vehicles are parked or loaded.

Be alert, be thorough - get to know the assignment that you are on, including the people you need to communicate with on a regular basis, and investigate anything out of the ordinary. You should check your assignment Instructions if you are not sure of the action to take in a situation.

Fire Hazards

Fire is the largest single cause of financial loss and damage to industry and commerce. A fire can put a company out of business. Prevention of fire is, therefore, one of the most important duties. It is necessary at this stage to identify what must be looked for regarding fire risks, whilst patrolling an assignment. People can be directly instrumental in causing fires in many ways. For example:

• Throwing cigarette ends into wastepaper baskets.

• Smoking in prohibited areas.

• Leaving equipment on that produces heat or flame, like blowtorches or welding guns.

• Ignoring works regulations and company rules, which specially relate to fire prevention.

• During the winter months leaving heating appliances on unintentionally, or in dangerous areas near inflammable material or gases.

• Leaving heating appliances in awkward places where they could be knocked over or putting objects on top of them.

People are also responsible for potential fire hazards in the following ways:

• Overloading circuits so that the ensuing electrical faults cause fires.

• Using old equipment that has either not been maintained or has been carelessly serviced.

• Using machinery that overheats because of inadequate ventilation.

There are many other examples that could be used. We stress the need to look for fire hazards especially during your first patrol. A routine like the following example would be useful.

Whilst On Your First Patrol:

• Close all fire doors to prevent a fire spreading from one compartment or section to another. Doors must also be closed to prevent the building from becoming smoke filled.

• Remove any obstructions in front of fire exit doors, fire alarms, extinguishers or hydrants.

• Where there are flammable materials, such as paint, combustible materials or where gas canisters are used or stored, you should make frequent visits of inspection. Be thorough in checking that all is safe.

• Note any accumulation of rubbish, or materials near boilers, stores, etc., and record this in the report book.

• Turn off all electric switches and remove plugs except those specified. Read your Assignment Instructions.

• Ensure that any bonfires or rubbish fires are properly extinguished.

• During the first patrol inspect all parts of the premises as soon as possible after they are vacated, systematically checking all the known danger points.

Flooding Hazards

Flooding is a major threat to property and equipment. Prevention of flooding is possible if you know what to look for and take the necessary immediate action. Common causes of flooding:

• Taps that have been left running in toilets, kitchenettes and canteens, etc.

• Leaks in plumbing systems or water tanks.

• Faulty air conditioning systems that result in flooding.

• Acts of God, such as heavy rain or snowfall.

On the first patrol you should check all areas where taps are present and areas where water or other fluids are stored. Remember, water always flows downwards, so check the lowest point of your assignment if flooding is suspected.

Use Of Senses

During patrolling duties your alertness and thoroughness could prevent any number of incidents. The level of professionalism that you may achieve may depend on how you make use of the following human senses: Sight, Hearing, Touch, Smell, Taste. The aim of this subsection is to reveal how you might use your senses. Your ability to prevent damage or loss depends on your ability to detect any problems before they can escalate.

• **Sight:** Your eyes are the most valuable sense that you have. Use them to look for: Fire hazards, signs of illegal or forced entry. Open or forced windows and doors. People still on the premises outside working hours. Unusual lighting. Signs of flooding or leaks. People acting suspiciously. Checking ID cards to satisfy yourself of a person's right to be on an assignment

• **Hearing:** Your ears are vitally important and can detect many things that the eye cannot. They can listen for: Sound of materials burning. Sounds of broken glass or forced entry. Footsteps, talking or other unusual noises. Running water or dripping taps. Machinery or equipment that is normally switched off. Anything out of the ordinary.

• **Touch:** Touch can be very useful whilst patrolling. Hands can be used to test temperatures of certain items of machinery or equipment particularly those, which are not normally warm. This may indicate overheating and a potential fire risk. Obviously, you must not touch any equipment, which could have reached a temperature high enough to burn the skin. You may walk into a room and immediately feel that it is too hot and look for the cause; vice versa - you may feel too cold in an area that is normally warm. The cause may be that a piece of machinery has broken down, or that the central heating system has failed. Also, unusual drafts, which may, on investigation, lead to discovery of open windows or doors.

• **Smell:** Your sense of smell is particularly useful with regard to fire hazards. The smell of burning provides an early warning that a fire may be breaking out. Or a smell of gas or paint fumes at odd times may indicate leakages and potential a disaster, if ignited. The smell of fuel may indicate a leak in fuel pumps or from vehicles.

• **Taste:** Unlike in the movies, do not taste anything!

Patrol Routes & Exclusion Areas

• **Patrol Routes:** Patrol routes through the areas of an assignment are sometimes laid down by the client but are more often or not left to the discretion of the patrolling guards. Unless stated in the assignment Instructions, patrol routes should be varied from time to time and the route changed so that a pattern is not apparent.

• **Exclusion Areas:** An exclusion area is a part of an assignment that the client wishes the guards to avoid altogether when patrolling the site. Both patrol routes and exclusion areas will be determined between the security company employing the guards and the company, which is paying for the guarding services. If the operative has any concerns with patrol routes, then he should address them through his team leader.

These are merely sensible basic rules to follow during patrols. Between scheduled full patrols, 'snap checks' should be made to one or two important key points such as a safe room, secondary entrances or other sensitive areas.

A snap check is a "mini' patrol to one or two specific areas of risk on the assignment; this helps to avoid any chance of potential intruders being certain about the timing of your patrols. The frequency of patrols will depend on the size and complexity of the assignment. It is a good idea to retrace your steps on some occasions and vary the route if this is acceptable to the client.

Always listen for a few moments before entering a premises or going into another area. Use soft-soled boots or shoes, if possible, to be able to patrol quietly without announcing your arrival. These are all good habits that an operative need to acquire.

The Initial Patrol

The initial patrol is the most important during the whole period of duty. The guard needs to satisfy himself that everything is normal around his assignment at the start of his duty. The first steps are: - Sign on for duty. Read the Report Book. Read the Assignment Instructions and check that there are no special messages or amendments. Once these procedures are complete the initial patrol can be started. Before doing your initial patrol follow personal fire precautions. This means stubbing out cigarette ends if you smoke, making sure any heating equipment being used is safe, and switching off the kettle in the security office! During this patrol several tasks need to be done, some of which are not repeated until the last patrol these include:

• Checking all external doors to ensure that they are locked.

• Checking that all windows are secure.

• Checking all internal doors, particularly fire and smoke doors to ensure they are closed.

• Checking all electrical appliances, switching off and unplugging any that are left on

• Checking all toilets and washrooms, ensuring that all taps are turned off and plugs are out of the sinks.

• Checking and switching off any unnecessary lights.

If all these checks are thorough, then taking the appropriate action will have prevented incidents/accidents. Take adequate time to satisfy yourself that any problems that do arise are not a result of something that was overlooked on the initial lengthened patrol. Detail any potential problems or incidents in the Report Book after the patrol are completed. The initial patrol should cover every inch of the assignment. Apart from the listed Exclusion Areas. After completing this patrol, further routine patrols and snap checks can be varied both in timing, length and the number of clocking points visited if a watchman's clock is in use. It is normal during routine patrols, that all clocking points are visited; these should be located in vulnerable areas around the assignment.

Action To Be Taken On Discovery Of An Irregularity

What do we mean by 'irregularity'? It is anything that is out of the ordinary or unusual and does not immediately constitute a crime. On discovering an irregularity whilst on patrol, there are various actions you could take. The course chosen depends on two things. A. Is a major problem or a small problem? B. What is the agreement with the client? For examples: - If a small leak is found in a kitchen water pipe during the night, the guard could put a bucket underneath it and report it to the client in the morning. On the other hand, if the guard finds a safe open, then it is likely that the client would need to be informed immediately, whatever the time, at night or in the day. In most cases any irregularity should be reported to the team leader and noted in the report book.

Scenes Of Crime

Whilst on duty it is likely that sooner or later you will discover a crime that has been committed. There are certain actions that you need to take in a calm and logical manner. The following incidents are examples of what you could find and what action you should take to deal with the situation and preservation any evidence. Whilst on patrol you find a small fire, which you successfully extinguish. There are matches scattered nearby and some charred paper that could have been to start the fire.

ACTION:

• Call the Fire Brigade in order that they can check that the fire is completely out.

• Contact your control room/office as soon as you can and tell them what has happened.

• Do NOT attempt to clear up the debris as this should be left for the Chief Fire Officer to examine.

• Do cordon off the area if there are other people on the site.

• Do make brief notes and videos of what happened, what you saw and did, together with timings.

On your second patrol of the premises, you find that a locked door has been forced and that some items appear to have been stolen.

ACTION:

• If there are other people on the site, inform the most senior.

• Do ensure that the Police have been informed.

• Do inform your control room/office as soon as possible.

• Do cordon off the area or block it off in some way, unless instructed otherwise.

• Do make brief notes of what happened, what you saw and did, together with timings.

During the hours of darkness, you find goods that you recognize as belonging to the client, hidden near the perimeter of the assignment

ACTION:

• Do leave the goods undisturbed (unless circumstances dictate otherwise).

• Do ensure that the Police are informed (unless instructed otherwise).

• Do inform your control room/office as soon as possible.

• DO cordon off the area or block it off in some way (unless instructed otherwise).

• Do keep observations on the goods if possible.

• Do make brief notes of what happened, what you saw and what you did, together with timings.

• Do listen carefully to instructions - you may be asked to keep careful observations on the scene, or you may be asked to wait until either or all the following arrive: - The Police, your team leader or client.

Your actions in all these cases may differ slightly from our examples according to who is present on the site and according to the company for whom you work. The principle however is the same. Approach the situation in a calm and logical manner, do not put yourself at risk, but do take the correct action. Record briefly what you saw, what you did and who was informed, together with timings. Remember - if an incident has occurred that will need investigation, it is important that you take steps to preserve and record evidence that needs to be commented on or produced later.

Summary

In this section you have learnt the basic rules and procedures of patrolling around an assignment. The principal hazards you may encounter in industry and commerce as regards to security of assignments, and the risk of damage and financial loss. How to use your sight, hearing, smell, touch and taste to identify and prevent incidents from developing into disasters. Patrol routes, snap checks, exclusion areas and patrol techniques. The reasons why the initial patrol needs extra time and care to prevent incidents and possible accidents. And what to do on finding something unusual, or what action to take in more serious incidents.

EXAMPLE OF INDUSTRIAL SECURITY SITE ORDERS

The following images are of a set of assignment orders (Assignment Instructions) for a sensitive manned security contract in the UK. This location and the security company that had the contract have long since shut down, so its OK for me to share the documents.

From what is listed below you will be able to see what should be included in professional site orders. Each set of site orders need to be adapted specifically to the locations, the needs of the client and the threats identified in the threat assessment. Site orders for a residence would of course be significantly different from those below due to the different nature of the threats, duties involved and locations.

Site Copy

ASSIGNMENT INSTRUCTIONS

These assignment instructions have been prepared to detail those aspects of the customer's contract that are specific to the client, and may be in addition to, or at variance with, the standard Quality System Procedures. Therefore, this document must be read in conjunction with any related company procedures.

ASSIGNMENT NAME AND ADDRESS

ASSIGNMENT TELEPHONE NUMBER

ASSIGNMENT FAX NUMBER

PERSONS RESPONSIBLE FOR SECURITY

Mr Kevin

OUT OF HOURS CONTACTS

THE FIRST POINT OF CONTACT FOR ANY PROBLEM IS MR KEVIN   OR THE DUTY ENGINEER. THEIR CONTACT NUMBERS CAN BE FOUND IN THE ASSIGNMENT LOG.

THIS INFORMATION IS STRICTLY CONFIDENTIAL AND MUST NOT BE DIVULGED TO ANYONE

CONTACT NUMBERS

DUTY CONTROLLER (17.30 to 09.30)

Head Office :
Telephone   :
Fax   :
E-Mail   :

DIRECTOR OF OPERATIONS -

MANAGING DIRECTOR

DIRECTOR

CHECK CALLS TO BE MADE <u>HOURLY</u> ON NIGHT SHIFT, AT WEEKENDS AND ON BANK HOLIDAYS

List of attachments:

OPERATIONS LOG
ASSIGNMENT LOG
CONTRACTORS BOOK
VISITORS BOOK

operate a Quality Management System to the requirements of BS EN ISO9002. Customers are requested to assist this process by approving and returning a copy of these instructions. Instructions not returned within 10 days of issue will be deemed acceptable.

Approved: ....
(On behalf of the Client)
Date: 3/6/97

Distribution:	Page 1 of 2
2 Copies to client (less attachments) - signed copy to be returned.	Issue: 2
1 Copy to site log - 1 Copy to Control Room (less attachments)	
1 Copy to Contract file (less attachments)	Review date: **APRIL 1998**

ASSIGNMENT INSTRUCTIONS

Hours of Work

Monday to Thursday	17.30 - 09.00 hours
Friday	17.30 - 07.00 hours
Saturday	07.00 - 19.00 hours
	19.00 - 07.00 hours
Sunday	07.00 - 19.00 hours
	19.00 - 09.00 hours } Including Bank Holidays

Manning Levels

1 Security Officer

PATROLLING

~~Random EXTERNAL patrol duties (frequency not specified)~~ *N.*

- Check computer rooms
- Check that windows are closed
- Check internal fire doors are closed
- Check lights are switched off
- Note and report obstructions in fire escapes routes
- Check that break glasses and fire appliances are operable
- Check for leaks - especially in toilets and vending areas
- Check all PAC security doors are functioning correctly
- Check fire phones, fire equipment, and panic buttons are operational
- Check kitchens

N.B. NO EXTERNAL PATROLS ARE TO BE MADE

UNDER NO CIRCUMSTANCES IS THE SECURITY OFFICER TO LEAVE THE BUILDING TO INVESTIGATE AN INCIDENT (OR FOR ANY OTHER REASON) IF HELP IS REQUIRED HE IS TO CALL ASSISTANCE FROM EITHER CONTROL OR THE EMERGENCY SERVICES

RECEPTION DUTIES

- Receive telephone calls and deal with client requests
- Liaise with　　　　　　　　　　 personnel
- Check visitors and contractors in and out of the premises
- Check in-coming 'by hand' deliveries
- Issue keys to authorised personnel

31

ORLANDO WILSON

PURPOSE

This procedure details the controls to be exercised in respect of Manned Guarding Assignments.

CONTENTS

General.
Assignment Report.
Assignment Instructions.
Incident reports.
Patrols.
Standing orders.

QUALITY RECORDS

Assignment Report.
Incident report.
Operations Book.
Supervisors Shift Report.
Assignment Instructions

MANNED SECURITY GUARDING	ISSUE: 1 PAGE 2 of 6

GENERAL

Each manned security site shall be issued with an Site Log Book which shall contain the following:
- **Assignment Reports**;
- Assignment Instructions;
- Blank **Incident Reports**

Term 'Controller' used in this procedure shall be read as:
Nights
Control Room
Days
Control Room - for Booking-on/off duty and Check Calls.
Director of Operations or Duty Manager - For occurrences, incidents or other emergencies (except which reports to Control Room).

Additionally, the management team may be contacted, in the event of emergencies, 24 hours per day.

Each site shall hold a **Operations Book** which shall be used to record all occurrences that are not anticipated or part of a routine. Details of the occurrence and the resulting action taken shall be summarised, as follows:
- Date;
- Entry - (Next sequential No, Details of occurrence and actions taken);
- Signature / Time.

ASSIGNMENT REPORT

At the start of duty the Security Officer shall initiate an **Assignment Report**, to cover the shift. This document could be considered a legal document in the event of a dispute and **must** be used to record all activities undertaken on behalf of the company and the client.

Occurrences and Incidents may be summarised with suitable crossed reference to the **Operations Book** entry and **Incident Report**, where applicable.

It is essential that activities and duties are entered as they occur, on no account must the entries be left and entered at the end of a shift.

If visiting supervision find this has happened, a Non-conformance and Corrective Action Report shall be issued and disciplinary action taken.

Assignment Reports shall be sent to Head Office on a monthly basis.

Note: Sites that are 'supervised' may have a specific **Supervisors Shift Report** developed to replace the **Assignment Report**. As the format and content of these will vary, to suit the needs of the site, they shall be developed as an attachment to the associated set of **Assignment Instructions**.

MANNED SECURITY GUARDING	ISSUE: 1
	PAGE 3 of 6

ASSIGNMENT INSTRUCTIONS

The Security Officer shall make him/herself aware of the **Assignment Instructions** and record this on the **Assignment Report**. Instructions that cannot be located or require clarification shall be reported to the Quality Representative.

In the event of the client giving instructions to vary any requirement, name or contact in the **Assignment Instructions**, details shall be recorded on the **Assignment Report**.

INCIDENT REPORTS

An incident is a serious occurrence that is not part of the routine (e.g. fire, break-in, assault or flooding). All incidents are to be recorded using the **Incident Report**, it is essential that the incident is fully documented. The report shall be completed as soon as practical after the incident and shall detail the times and sequence of events.

The Security Officer shall take the most appropriate course of action in respect of each incident, including notification to the controller and the emergency services, where applicable.

The Security Officer shall, at all times, avoid placing him/herself at risk.

Depending on the nature of an 'Incident', the report may become the basis of a claim by the company or the client.

Remember if in doubt raise an **Incident Report**.

Incident Reports shall be submitted to Head Office at the earliest opportunity. Copies may be given to the client's representative, where appropriate. The original shall be retained in the Site Log Book for a minimum of 3 months and then may be destroyed.

Note: Certain clients require **Incident Reports** to be presented in a different format to the company standard, in such cases these will be developed as attachments to the associated assignment instructions.

PATROLS

Patrols shall be carried out to the times and frequency detailed in the **Assignment Instructions**, the times and duration being recorded on the **Assignment Report**.

| MANNED SECURITY GUARDING | ISSUE: 1 |
| | PAGE 4 of 6 |

STANDING ORDERS

The following standing orders form the principal procedures and duties of all Security Officers and unless varied to meet the requirements of particular assignments, are to be adhered to at all times.

Objectives:
- To protect the property of the client against fire, theft, damage and intruders.
- To ensure that no unauthorised persons or vehicles enter the clients premises and that those who are authorised are courteously dealt with.
- To ensure that no personnel including contractors, or any vehicle leaves the clients premises in an irregular manner.
- To render any assistance to the client or his personnel in any emergency.
- To record fully any unusual occurrence or incident as required.
- If breaches of industrial discipline, including infringement of the Health and Safety at Work Act are observed, action is to be confined to immediately reporting the matter to the clients representative and recording as above. Only if there is immediate risk and danger should the Security Officer intervene.
- Personal searches are not to be carried out without prior agreement in writing.
- Security Officers will be punctual in commencing their tour of duty and be in a fit and proper condition for their duties. They must not leave their assignment without permission or until relieved in the normal way.
- Every effort must be made to notify the controller as early as possible of impending absenteeism so that a relief can be arranged.
- If possible, Security Officers absent through sickness or other reasons shall inform the controller of their intended return at the earliest opportunity.
- Security Officers are to familiarise themselves with all assignment instructions. Variations to such instructions given by control or the client shall be recorded on the **Assignment Report**.
- Security Officers shall abide by any customer site specific rules (e.g. No smoking policy);
- Upon commencement of duty, Security Officers shall confirm the accuracy of records relating to customer property (e.g. Key Registers);
- All instructions to Security Officers are deemed to be confidential and must only be imparted to those with a 'need to know'. Any infringement without good reason will be considered a disciplinary offence.
- The Security Officer is in a privileged position within a client's organisation and may in such circumstances have knowledge which is confidential to the client. Such knowledge must be treated as above

MANNED SECURITY GUARDING	ISSUE: 1
	PAGE 5 of 6

Basic functions of a Security Officer:
- To carry out the duties as detailed in the Assignment Instructions.
- To carry out duties as verbally issued by .... Representatives or clients on our behalf.
- To safeguard the client's employees and property from Fire, Flood, Theft, Trespass, Vandalism and any other risk.
- To prevent accidents by reporting faulty equipment or hazard, in the line of Health & Safety Regulations.
- To record all occurrences, however minor they may seem, in the **Operations Book** and **Assignment Report**.
- To report all incidents to the controller with details being recorded via an **Incident Report**.
- To work in a manner that is safe both to themselves and other persons as required under Health and Safety Legislation.
- Ensure that any probationer at the assignment is familiar with standing orders and the assignment procedures.

Site Log Book :
- Your **Assignment Report** must be used to record all that happens whilst you are on duty, this is to include time on/off duty, receipt of clients keys, times check calls are made, out and in patrol times , plus all occurrences that effect security.
  All occurrences must be recorded in the **Assignment Report** and **Operations Book**. A serious occurrence shall be recorded in detail on an **Incident Report** with an entry of reference made on the **Assignment Report**.
- Entries must be in Blue or Black ink and be written clearly and precisely in plain English.

Book On/Off Procedures:
- Security Officers, on unsupervised sites, arriving for duty must 'Book-on' with the controller personally.
- Always ensure you 'Book-on' at the correct time, clearly stating your name. (Any Officers booking on after the official start time will be booked on at time of call and will only receive payment from that time).
- Security Officers who are not relieved by an oncoming guard, within 15 minutes of their shift ending, must notify control. The Officer shall remain on site until relieved, and notify control of the time of relief.

Check Calls:
- Security Officers, on unsupervised sites, are required in accordance with Health & Safety policies to make Check Calls. These are to give an assurance that both you and the premises you are guarding are safe.
- Check Calls must be made at the prescribed time you are allocated, and at the correct frequency allotted to your assignment.
- On making a Check Call, you must state your name clearly, also mentioning anything untoward that may have occurred since your last call.
- Failure to make a Check Call will result in a call from the controller after a waiting period and a possible visit by a duty manager if no response is gained or if the controller feels that the respondent is not Bona Fide. The Police may also be informed and requested to attend site.

MANNED SECURITY GUARDING	ISSUE: 1
	PAGE 6 of 6

Radio use:
- Assignments that have two-way radios must have them switched on at all times.
- Radios are only to be used for routine or emergency calls and not for conversation purposes between guards.
- All calls over radio must commence with your call sign directed to the call sign you require.

Uniform Dress:
- Security Officers when on duty must be in the company uniform, or that specified by the client.
- Black plain shoes or boots must be worn.
- Ties must always be worn.
- Epaulettes must always be worn on shirts or NATO jumpers.
- Full uniform must be worn at all times whilst on duty, any guards found to be not wearing uniform will be subject to disciplinary procedures.
- Uniforms must remain in a clean and tidy state, a clean and pressed shirt shall be worn for each shift, any defective item must be reported to Head Office for replacement.
- I.D. Cards are part of company uniform and must be worn or carried at all times whilst on duty.
- No weapons 'real' or 'imitation' will be carried on duty. Not even for self defence.
- Security Officers must be freshly shaved before commencing duty.

Disciplinary matters:
Listed below are some examples which, if not adhered to, will lead to disciplinary action and possible dismissal from the company.
- Failure to be dressed in proper uniform.
- Poor time keeping.
- Poor standard of work.
- Unauthorised, unreasonable and/or repeated absences (this can include certified sickness).
- Unauthorised presence at work.
- Disruptive behaviour.
- Smoking in any other than authorised areas.
- Abusive or insulting language.
- Fighting with, or injury to a fellow member of the company.
- Drinking of alcohol on duty or just prior to commencement of duty.
- Taking of non-prescribed drugs on duty or prior to duty.
- Leaving an assignment without proper relief or permission from the controller.
- Sleeping on duty.
- Damage, theft or neglect of company or client's property.
- Breach of Health & Safety or Hygiene Policies.
- Use of client's telephones for personal use.
- Allowing access to client's premises of unauthorised persons.
- Use of client's equipment without prior permission.
- Breach of either client or company confidentiality.

ROOM & BUILDING SEARCHES

You need to know how to search a room for IED's, electronic surveillance and contraband. By contraband I mean things like illegal drugs or weapons that could have been left in say, your hotel room by the previous occupant or planted in your office to cause you problems.

If you're hosting a business meeting, you should search and secure the room well in advance. If you are meeting at a client's location suggest to them, they should search the meeting room, if this would not be appropriate be aware of the possible threats and have procedures to counter them in place. When you have learned the basic procedures of how to search a room, you can search a whole building, the only difference being that it will take much longer to do so.

The first thing you need to consider when you're going to search a room, or a building is your personal security, as always you must be aware of your environment. If you are going into a room or building which has been left unoccupied always have someone watching your back, you never know who may be hiding in there.

Before you search the room or building you must first check the general area. Outside you want to be looking for people sat in parked cars or unattended vans, as these could be used for receiving or relay points for listening devices and cameras. Where possible you should always check the rooms above, below and around the room, you are going to search for anything suspicious.

You should clear everyone from the room or building before the search begins, then secure the area and only allow access to authorized personnel. Over the years I have seen meeting and function rooms being search while the venue staff was still setting up the rooms, bringing in furniture and food etc. This was a waste of time, the room or building needs to be secured, everyone cleared out before the search begins. Then everyone entering meeting room's needs to be searched, even if they are re-entering after having just left, to say use the bathroom or smoke a cigarette.

What you are looking for when you search a room will depend on your threat assessment. Not everyone will face the threat of IED's but maybe the threat of electronic surveillance or just staying in a hotel room that had questionable guests before them.

So, let's say you have searched the outside of the room and are now going to make entry. First you should make a visual inspection of the door, looking for anything suspicious such as signs of forced entry, also use your senses to try to smell or hear anyone or any thing in the room before you make entry.

To search a doorway, look around it for anything attached to it and then look just inside for any wires or thread or anything that might be a laser or electric sensor. Do not open a door fully, do so slowly and always check behind the door and at the hinges, as this is a good place for a pressure switch for a booby trap to be placed. Now you must check the floor just inside the door; doorways are channels and are good locations to place IEDs, as someone will eventually walk through there! If there is a mat you will need to lift it, if there is carpet or wood floors, you will need to check to see if there are any signs that they have been lifted.

When you enter the room don't turn on any lights until the switches and light fixtures have been checked for IEDs. Light switches and fixtures are also a favored place for listening devises as they can transmit indefinitely due to their power source being the mains.

If the room has windows close any blinds, you don't want others to see what you're doing. You should now remove all trash and furniture that's not needed for the meeting from the room; excess furniture means there are more places to hide listening devices and gives you more to search. If you think something could be suspicious or you don't have time to search it, then get it out of the room.

Now how the search continues will depend on the threat, how much time and manpower you have. If time is short, have a quick scan around the room for anything obvious; check under tables, chairs and behind pictures etc. This may seem too obvious, but I have caught out many a student by placing a key box under their chair. Think like the criminals; if you had a couple of minutes to place a device, where would you put it?

When time permits you should do a more detailed search. Let's say you're going to be using a hotel suite as a meeting room, and you will need to search it by yourself. As always, your personal security is priority, so when you're in the suite, lock and secure the door and keep any weapons you may have at hand.

Start by doing a 360-degree search of the walls and make note and investigate any signs of recent building work or renovation, be on the lookout for any small holes that could have miniature cameras or microphones in them. Remove and search any pictures, check all electrical and phone sockets, check any heaters or air conditioning units. Windows would need to be checked inside and out, make sure to also check any blinds and curtains.

You will then need to check the floor, the ceiling or roof; inspect the flooring for any signs of interference, if there are false ceiling panels you'll have to get up there and check what's between them and the roof. All furniture, bookcases, cabinets, couches, seats, ornaments, potted plants, all electrical items would need to be taken apart and searched. As you should be beginning to see a thorough room search can take a long time, so remove as much stuff as possible before you start the search!

Other places that criminals can use to conceal contraband etc. include any hollow and removable items such as inside the curtain rods for windows or showers, clothes hanger rails inside wardrobes and inside toilet cisterns. Also, most doors these days are hollow so, if a hole is made in the top contraband can be hidden inside; always run your hand across a top of a door.

This chapter is just to get you thinking, searching rooms and buildings can take a very long time if done properly. Professional search teams usually arrive at a location with sniffer dogs and a van load of equipment to be able to unscrew everything in sight. As a lone traveler at most you may have a Swiss army knife or multipliers and a flashlight. Make these parts of your travel equipment and learn how to utilize them.

In addition to working out your search procedures you need to work out what you'll do if you find an explosive device, a listening device or contraband. Think about it, if you find a kilo of cocaine in your room are you going to go to the police and tell them it's not yours? Think they'll believe you? Or are you just going to change hotels without leaving your fingerprints on the package? All depends on where you are in the world, and your threat assessment!

EMERGENCY & CRISIS PLANNING

Professional emergency and crisis planning is what prevents potential problems from turning into disasters. All emergency and crisis planning needs to be kept simple and relevant to the problems they are trying to prevent or minimize. All procedures need to be rehearsed so everyone is clear on what they need to do in an emergency, talking about it is not enough. Plans discussed in comfortable meeting rooms will be enacted in a completely different manner when people are under stress, frightened and things around them are going wrong.

One thing to remember when drawing up your emergency and crisis plans is the simple truth that in reality everything will most likely go wrong. Therefore, you must try to keep your plans as simple and flexible as possible; your plans must be able to adapt to very fluid situations.

Over the years I have come across quite a few "experts" who have drawn up crisis plans for large business and government facilities that were completely unrealistic. One national organization, which had a contract with a local authority, contacted us to put together a 4-hour program designed to train unarmed county security personnel and bus drivers in anti-terrorist and hostage rescue techniques. It took numerous conversations for them to understand it takes more than 4 hours to train a SWAT team and it helps if the students have a little bit of experience. Teaching such techniques to untrained, unfit and inexperienced people simply increases the chances that if there was ever a hostage incident, they would do nothing more than escalate the situation and cause unnecessary casualties. These things are best left to the professionals.

Here are some basic considerations for putting an emergency or crisis management team and plan together for your business or facility.

Team Formation

If you need to put together a crisis team, everyone should know their responsibilities within the team and emphasis any special skills they can offer to the group.

Possible responsibilities of team members could include:

- Team commander
- Sub-commanders
- Dealing with medical emergencies
- Dealing with legal issues
- Media relations
- Security and conflict resolution
- Liaison with outside agencies
- Evacuation and lock down coordination
- Transport and vehicle marshalling
- Search and rescue
- After incident therapy

The Threat Assessment

You will need to compile a threat assessment and identify any potential threats that you or your organization may be under. You will also need to consider what assets and personnel you have available to deal with the threats. Threats could include:

- Traffic problems
- Drug use or dealing

- Workplace or domestic violence
- Suicides or suicide attempts
- Indecent behavior/sexual predators
- Fire or flooding
- Natural disasters (tornados/hurricanes/earthquakes)
- Theft or loss of assets
- Intruders
- Explosive devices
- Terrorist attacks
- Kidnapping/hostage situations
- Chemical incidents

Basic things you need to consider when dealing with an incident:

• **Communications and incident reporting:** How is the alarm going to be raised and who is going to report to whom?

• **Alerting relevant parties:** How are the relevant personnel for that incident going to be alerted?

• **Incident reaction:** How are you going to deal with that incident?

There is no way I can tell you how to react to every incident, but, based upon my experience, you can expect each one to be different. I'll try to give you some guidelines to make you think, so you can develop your own strategies that are relevant to your own situations.

Here are some considerations if you are putting together emergency plans for a residence or office building. If there is a situation such as an improvised explosive device being found close to your location, you will have two basic choices: You can either stay in the building or evacuate. What you do will depend on the size and location of the device and what your building is made of.

If you choose to evacuate, you should consider:

• How will everybody be alerted to the incident?

• What are the staff responsibilities at all levels, and do those assigned responsibilities know what they are doing?

• Does everyone know the evacuation procedures for their area of the building and what exits will be used?

• Does everyone know where to go after evacuating the building?

• How will everyone be accounted for?

• Will transport be needed to get staff away from the building to a safe area?

• What first aid and emergency help will be available?

• How will people disperse after the incident?

If you choose to stay in the building, you should consider:

• How will the order for a lock down be issued to everyone?

• What are the staff responsibilities at all levels?

• Do those who are assigned responsibility know what they are doing?

• Does everyone know where the safe areas are within the building?

• How will people be alerted that the incident is over or that they need to evacuate the building?

The above is just a guide to get you thinking, emergency and crisis planning is a very detailed job. There is more to it than printing a form from the internet and just ticking a few boxes!

THREAT ASSESSMENTS (TA)

The Threat Assessment (TA) is the most important of all the procedures carried out in any security or business operation but even the most basic TAs are regularly overlooked. The reason for a TA is to identify anything that might threaten you, your team and your overall operation. People carry out basic forms of TAs all the time: Which bars are safe to drink in, where is it safe to walk at night, do I need locks on the windows of my home etc.

A threat assessment must identify all threats that you are exposed to whether it is physical assault, injury, terrorism, black mail, being embarrassed or discredited, health problems, loss of assets or dangerous weather conditions etc. When you identify a threat, you must take procedures to minimalize it. In the world of security operations, most people only look for the threat of physical assault, but you must look as deeply as you can and cover every angle.

Consider this, a security company is looking after a client who is being threatened by a potentially violent ex-business partner. The client is married with children. The children have several pets: a cat and a dog. The client lives in a two-story house surrounded by a garden. The security company has identified the threat and decided to install CCTV and provide the client with a team of armed bodyguards. The ex-business partner decides to strike at the client. One night he throws bits of meat he has poisoned over the wall into the client's garden, which the client's pets eat. When the client and his family wake up in the morning, the pets are dead, and his children are very upset. 1-0 to the opposition. Could this have been avoided, maybe, maybe not. I doubt that many people would consider that a client's family pets would need to be considered in a TA. As I am sure you will agree, such an attack as I have described would be a psychological assault on the client and by upsetting his family would most probably have more of an effect than just physically assaulting him.

When first compiling a TA, you need to get as much information as possible, past, present and future on the person or organization on whom you will be compiling the assessment. Most people may not want to include certain things like extra marital affairs, drug or drinking habits or similar activities. However, it is vitally important that these are included, as they are a source of many potential problems. It would make sense in a lot of business operations to compile and profile staff and family members.

When you compile the threat assessment and a threat is identified, you must find out as much about it as is possible-whether it is an illness or organized criminals. You will need to locate sources of information for your research including media cuttings, libraries, trade catalogues, directories, public records and the Internet. You need to assess what action has been taken against you from a threat: verbal abuse, physical assault, stealing trash, tapping your phones or previous heart attacks.

If the information compiled is used properly it can help you to predict the criminal's plan of action, and it will also aid law enforcement agencies in apprehending them. I have included below a crime prevention assessment on a residence; from this you should be able to see things that need to be taken into consideration when compiling threat assessments. Remember, all TA and profiles need to be kept strictly confidential.

Below is an example of an assessment that was compiled on an apartment complex in Miami Beach after one of the units was broken into several times, and the tenants were considering suing the owner for security negligence.

Example Of A Basic Residential Threat Assessment

Date: ## /## /####   File Number: #########

Location: Apt ##, ## ###### Miami Beach, FL, 33###

The front of the building, East Side

The front entrance to the building is completely open with no visible security or deterrents to trespassers. Anyone can walk off the street and up to the apartments.

Possible procedures that could be put in place to deter trespassers include:

• Properly placed lights that illuminate all dark areas. The evening, I viewed the building, there were lights out in one of the stairways; this could also be a safety concern for tenants/guests and a liability concern for the building management.

• Security cameras could be placed to cover the main entrance or dummy security cameras could be placed in obvious locations to act as a deterrent to possible trespassers.

• Signs could be placed in obvious locations stating that the building has security cameras, and trespassers will be prosecuted, etc.

Rear and side perimeters

There did not seem to be any fences or barriers around the building that could stop a possible trespasser. The walls and fences would be easy to climb or cross for the average person.

Possible procedures that could be put in place to deter trespassers include:

• Properly placed lights, possibly on motion detectors can be placed in all dark areas.

• As with the front of the building, cameras and signs can be used to deter possible trespassers.

• The perimeter fencing needs to be replaced with something that will stop trespassers. There is no point having locked gates, if people can just jump a wall or fence a few yards away.

Walkways: There is nothing stopping people walking from the

street onto the 1st floor walkways. Lockable gates could possibly be placed at the bottom of the steps leading to the walkways.

Apartments

• The doors of the apartments need to be fitted with good locks and inspected to ensure that the locks cannot be opened through a nearby window. The door frames also need to be inspected to ensure they are solid. All locks on external doors need to be changed after tenants' leases are expired and before new tenants take over the apartment; I believe this is required under Florida law.

• The apartment windows are in no way secure and are easily opened from the outside. These windows need to be replaced.

• The shutters on the inside of the windows could be alarmed and would provide warning for occupants of an intruder gaining access to the apartment. The shutters themselves are flimsy and could not stop anyone trying to gain access to the apartment, but some form of dead bolt could be put in place to deter anyone from using excessive force to gain entry.

• Internal alarms could be used but it must be remembered these only alert others during a break-in, they do not prevent break-ins. If alarms are to be put in place, they must be serviced and tested regularly.

Conclusion

In my professional opinion, the building and the apartments' security level is extremely low. I personally would not be comfortable leaving valuable assets or having close friends, etc., living in the building. The main weakness is the easy accessibility to the apartments from the street and the ease of access to the apartments that can be gained through the windows.

These days with crime rates on the increase the building management and landlords need to understand that they are legally liable for the security and safety of their tenants.

DETAILED BUILDING SURVEY

Here is a template for a detailed building security survey in potentially hostile environments. As you read through you will see that some of the things mentioned will not be applicable if you are assessing the security for a business, house or apartment in areas where there is low level crime and no serious active threats. As I said earlier, use this as a guide and take what is useful for you.

1. Identification

a. Local and Official Name (from map study).

b. General Location and Address.

c. Map References. Identify by map series, sheet number, and edition.

d. Grid references and GPS coordinates

e. Additional Information. Indicate any peculiar information, date of original survey, and any updates if applicable.

2. Surrounding Area

a. General Information.

(1) General overview. Include aerial photograph{s}.

(2) Map references.

(3) Additional information.

b. Tactical Considerations.

(1) Command posts (CP's). Include the following information:

(a) Entrance(s) and approach routes.

(b) Security, cover, and concealment.

(c) Provisions for water, electricity, telephone, ventilation, rest rooms, adequate working space, and satellite communications antennas.

(d) Who owns the building, the address, the point of contact (POC), facilities available in the area, and vehicle and foot approach routes to the building. (Ensure the CP is shown on the surrounding area sketch, and if possible, show photographs of the building and area.)

(2) Surveillance/sniper positions. Include the following.

(a) An overwatch of the area.

(b) Concealed access routes to the CP and staging areas.

(c) Secured and concealed accesses and/or entrances to the surveillance position.

(d) Cover and concealment of the surveillance position from observation by personnel located on the location.

(e) Provisions for water, electricity, and restroom facilities.

(f) The location of the surveillance position on the surrounding area sketch. (Show photographs of the building in which the surveillance position is located, the surveillance position in the building, the view from the surveillance position to the location, and the view from the location to the surveillance position.)

(g) A description of the following: 1. Type of building. 2. Number of stories. 3. Location of surveillance position in relation to the location. 4. The area to be used by the observer. 5. Who owns the building, address, POC(s), and their telephone numbers. 6. Access routes to the area.

(3) Staging areas. Include the following:

(a) Whether the structure has a basement or other large area concealed from outside view.

(b) If the staging area is in the vicinity of the location preferably in the surrounding area.

(c) Suitability for holding number of personnel for how many days.

(d) Provisions for water, electricity, and rest rooms available, if possible.

(e) Whether routes to the CP are concealed from observation by personnel located on the location.

(f) Concealment of accesses (for example, underground parking lot}.

(g) The location of the staging area in relationship to the location, who owns the building, POC for access and his telephone number, recommended approaches to the area, and recommended entrances. (Show the location of the staging area on the surrounding area sketch and photographs of the building and the area.)

(4) Recommended approaches. Include the following:

(a) Main direction from the staging area to the location and surveillance positions.

(b) Whether approach is by air, land, or water.

(c) Whether it is by vehicle or foot.

(d) Any unusual circumstances about the approach (for example, an approach over rooftops of surrounding buildings, facilities such as banks located near the approach that may have 24-hour guards).

(e) Blind or insecure spots on the approaches.

(f) If possible, photographs of the route from the staging area to the location along the recommended approach.

(5) Sanctuaries. Include the following information:

(a) Friendly government embassies, churches or residences in the area.

(b) The building and the area to be used as the sanctuary.

(c) Who owns the building, the address, the POC and telephone number(s), location in relation to the location, and what the facility is normally used for.

(d) Location of the sanctuary in relation to helicopter landing zones (LZ's) and evacuation routes.

(e) Location of the structure on the surrounding area sketch. (Show photographs of the building and, if possible, of the area to be used as sanctuary.)

(6) Obstacles and/or danger areas. Include the following information:

(a) Vegetation and terrain surrounding the location.

(b) Open areas (for example, large avenues adjacent to the location).

(c) Locations of guarded banks or other guarded facilities, hostile country embassies, and threat group offices.

(d) High crime areas and the most common type of criminal occurrence in these areas.

(e) Roadways or avenues recommended for approaches that are affected by rush hour traffic.

(f) Checkpoints, curfews, police or security patrols, universities, construction areas, police or military installations.

(g) Exceptionally well illuminated areas around the location.

3. Ground description

(a) General Description. Always orient the direction of the survey to main geographical points. Pay particular attention to basic locations, type of construction, distances from perimeter barriers to principal structures and then structures of a secondary nature to the principal structures.

(b) Perimeter Barrier. Total information coverage is required. Emphasize heights, widths, and thicknesses. Zero in on weak spots and describe them in detail.

(c) Entrances to Grounds. Examine points of normal or prepared access, style of construction, security and/or locking devices, closed-circuit televisions (CCTV's), and guards.

(d) Structures. Include any additional structures located on the grounds.

(e) Terrain and Vegetation. Provide a very simple description (for example, height and type of trees).

(f) Additional Information. Include possible routes of access and masking effect of vegetation.

4. Building description

a. Exterior. Give a general description to include basic style of construction. Refer to aerial photographs, if available.

b. Entrances to Building. Give a detailed description including names of entrances, if applicable.

(1) Main entrances. Working from outside to inside, describe the entrance and any entrance procedures, if applicable. Describe hinges from the top down.

(2) Other entrances. Describe the same as above.

(3) Emergency entrances and exits. Describe the same as above.

(4) Additional information. Include grates, air conditioning ducts, fans, and trap doors,

c. Interior Description of Building.

(1) General description.

(2) Floor plans. Refer to attached floor plans and floor plan sketches.

(3) Floors. Include type of construction of the floors from the basement up.

(4) Corridors. State width, height, type of lighting, type of floor covering, depths of doorways, and general information.

(5) Stairways. Describe by name if possible and describe the locations of landings and banisters. Give the number of stairs.

(6) Elevators. Include mechanism, escape hatch, and other contents of the elevator (off the data plate) including any limitations of the elevator (for example, that it does not service the top floor).

(7) Doors and locks. Refer to a specific industry or professional standard door/lock/key chart available to all participating organizations.

(8) Windows and locks. Describe standard type(s) for the specific structure and any exceptions.

(9) Physical barriers. Describe any barrier system that will be used during an emergency.

(10) Hardened areas. Describe in detail.

(11) Weak points. Describe in detail.

(12) Additional information. Describe in detail.

d. Roof.

(1) General description. List antennas, elevator rooms, and type of construction.

(2) Entrances and exits. Describe in detail, with emphasis on areas of weak construction.

(3) Fire escapes and ladders. Describe in detail.

5. Common Systems

a. Security.

(1) Personnel.

(a) Security guards. Give the numbers, are they competent and types of weapons carried.

(b) Security detail and/or bodyguard. Describe the same as above.

(c) Contract watchmen. Give the numbers, are they competent, types of weapons, and times of shift changes.

(d) National policemen. Give the numbers, are they competent and affiliation with the facility.

(2) Total security equipment. Include a total inventory of all security equipment.

(3) Sensors and alarms.

(a) Location outside.

(b) Location inside.

(c) Communications.

(d) Organic Transportation.

(e) Medical Equipment.

(f) Power. (1) Explain primary, normal system (for example, source and shutoff data). (2) Explain backup and emergency system(s) (for example, source, shutoff data, and duration capability). (3) Provide additional information. (4) Air Conditioning and Ventilation. Explain the air conditioning system, with special emphasis on vents and air intakes. (5) Sewage and Drainage. Explain the sewage system that services the structure with a special emphasis on access to the structure, if any. (6) Additional Information.

6. Personnel Structure

a. Staffing Pattern.

b. Key Personality Data.

c. Additional Information.

(1) Draw north arrows on the photographs and annotate items of importance on them. Do not annotate on a photograph an item indicated on the legend and/or label, unless necessary.

(2) Assemble finished product in the following order: (a) Table of contents. (b) Narrative description. (c) Surrounding area sketch. (d) Photograph and/or slide index. (e) Photographs with labels,

north arrows and annotations. (f) Slides.

(3) Have another person check for accuracy.

NOTE. Attached as an enclosure should be the door/lock/key reference information. The standard format for the door system should be very simple and not require a great deal of time either to collect information against or to produce a survey from. The survey should be specifically prepared: 1. List all doors. 2. Note whether they are standard or not, giving a definition of what a "standard door" for that particular structure is. 3. Describe any door that is not standard

ELECTRONIC SURVEILLANCE

Electronic surveillance is a main intelligence gathering resource for governments, criminals, terrorists and private investigators. You need to understand that you can employ electronic surveillance when you are targeting others but, it can also be used against you!

It is easy to get hold of listening devices (bugs), bugging equipment and covert cameras from commercial outlets and the many shops that specialize in making and supplying this type of equipment. Today, many bugs and covert cameras can be hidden in almost any objects like books, computers, mobile phones, rocks, and clothing. You should always take precautions against bugs and covert cameras, especially when you are staying in hotels or moving into a new residence.

There are thousands of devices on the commercial market that claim to be able to detect bugs. However, bugs work on many different frequencies or on GSM networks and many commercially available bugs and bug detectors work on only a small sector of frequencies available. A professional criminal or terrorist will always try to use bugs that are outside of the usual frequencies or on GSM networks, so they stand less chance of detection. In addition, you must take into consideration remote-controlled bugs that can be turned on and off by the listener. With most equipment, you would not pick up this type of bug, because it would usually be turned off until needed, such as during a meeting. In this sector, the most expensive equipment is not always the best. If you consider buying it, make sure it does what the maker claims.

If your threat is from electric surveillance (ES), you should employ the services of a trusted specialist in the electronic counter-surveillance (ECM) field. Always check the credentials of the person you employ for this task and make sure he is trustworthy, also check out that his ECM kit is of a professional standard. An ECM specialist should also have the equipment that is required to find bugs that are not within the usual frequency ranges. If you use the services of a commercial ECM specialist, they must never be left unsupervised. There have been many cases where de-buggers have been found to be working for the opposition and planting or ignoring devices.

You should also be aware of the threat from "hard-wire" devices. These do not transmit information via the airways and cannot be detected by scanners, etc. A listen through a wall device is a good example of this type of device. The device could be placed on the outside of a meeting/hotel room and will pick up all the conversations taking place in the room. The device could be attached directly to a recorder, so there are no transmissions. There are government agencies claiming to have a microfiber device that they can stretch for 3 kilometers and receive good quality audio and video footage.

It would be unrealistic for you to always carry around with you ECM equipment. The best defense you have against these devices is to perform a physical search whenever you will be staying for some time in a room or moving into a new residence. You should always carry with you such equipment as a flashlight and a Swiss Army knife or type of tool. These basic items are all you should need to adequately perform a basic room search. If you anticipate that you will have to do an in-depth search, always take a full search kit.

How A Bug Could Be Placed

Consider this scenario: a criminal is targeting an executive for kidnapping. He needs to get information on the executive's movements, routine, etc. A simple tactic would be to place a listening device in the reception area of the target's office. The criminal would need to buy a simple, small listening device which could be bought over the internet or from a spy shop. The criminal would then task an associate, preferably female, to enter the reception area and ask the receptionists for directions, etc. While talking to the receptionists the female could blow her nose and ask them to let her put her tissue in their trash can. Wrapped in the tissue would be the bug. Who would ever ask to check a tissue someone has just blown their nose in! All going well the bug would now be in place and would pick up everything the receptionists are saying. Think about it, receptionists handle a lot of sensitive information: they make appointments, book taxis and restaurants, etc. A small bug could transmit for about 20 to 75 meters depending on its quality and the environment it's used in. If someone could not covertly get close enough to listen to it, a receiver attached to a digital voice activated recorder could be placed close by, in a flower bed or up a drainpipe, etc. GSM bugs use SIM cards so they can be listened to globally from any location with a phone connection.

Considerations

• Why might your client be under electronic surveillance?

• Who is the threat?   Criminal, government, commercial, personal?

• What is the expected level of skill and equipment of the opposition?

• What information about you does the opposition have?

Counter Procedures

• Change meeting rooms and places at short notice- this will cause problems for anyone who was planning to put you under electronic surveillance.

• Search rooms prior to meetings.

• Clear everyone from the room/area before the search and then secure the area and allow access to authorized personnel only after the search is finished.

• Upgrade the security of all areas and employ your own personnel in a counter-surveillance role.

• Physically search the area for suspect vehicles which could be used as a receiving/relay point for transmissions from a bug.

• Leave enough time to search the area before the meeting starts.

• Meeting rooms should have minimal furniture as this gives the opposition fewer places to plant bugs.

• Search everyone entering meeting rooms for recorders or transmitters and make sure all rubbish is searched and removed.

• Check any vacant-adjoining buildings and physically search the outside of buildings.

• Perform counter-surveillance physical and electronic during meetings.

• Keep a frequency scanner on permanent scan.

• Be aware of remote-controlled bugs.

• Search pictures, sockets, phones, plugs, any gifts. Place tape over screw heads, check any new furnishings, check ceiling panels, check outside the room.

• Draw curtains or close blinds before those attending the meeting enter the room.

Cell/mobile phones can also be used as listening devices when set to auto-answer. Once they are put in place the threat just calls the phone to hear what is being said in the close vicinity around the phone. The only limitations cell phones have, are their size and battery life. The other issue with cell/mobile phones is that they can be hacked or have surveillance apps installed. There are many commercially available surveillance apps for cell/mobile phone monitoring. In high-crime areas where the criminals are working with the police and cell phone companies, they can monitor your calls and e-mails via the servers.

Another cover for planting electronic surveillance devices are burglaries. If you came home and found that your house or car had been broken into, would you be more worried about what had been stolen or what had been put in place? If your car, house or hotel room has been broken into they need to be searched for electronic surveillance devices and contraband. I mentioned cars here because they are favored areas to plant listening devices as they are generally easier for the criminal or private investigator to get access to and break into than a residence. Also, consider what you discuss in your car; many an extramarital affair has been discovered or confirmed by a voice-activated Dictaphone placed in a straying spouse's car.

Dictaphones on their own can be used by criminals as listening devices. When combined with a miniature microphone (that can be bought from most electronics stores) they make an excellent hardwire device. Dictaphones these days can record more than seventy-two hours and the data transfers easily to a computer. Consider how easy it would be for a criminal to get access to the outside walls or roof of the location you're in right now!!! Drill a small hole through to the inside and then place the microphone in the hole. Outside, the microphone wire could be camouflaged and the Dictaphone waterproofed and concealed, even buried. Then, every few days, the criminal could come by and swap the Dictaphone for one with fresh batteries and memory. The only way to find such a device would be a physical search; the $25K bug locator and the $500 an hour specialist would be nothing more than a waste of time and money.

Hopefully, after reading this chapter, you are more aware of the threat from electronic surveillance and how easy it is for even low-level criminals to use this means of gathering intelligence on an intended target.

BUGGING CONSIDERATIONS

The below notes were given to me years ago by someone who had worked for government agencies in the 1970's and 1980's. It's a list of considerations for planting electronic surveillance devices. Before everything went digital, staged burglaries were used as a cover for planting electronic listening devices and gathering non-admissible evidence. So, if a location has been burglarized or a car broken into, think about what could have been put in place, not just what's stolen.

- What information is needed?
- Where can we get it?
- Who from?
- Is there any other means of obtaining the information without bugging?
- If a bug is to be placed, then where, HOME, WORK, or VEHICLE?
- What are the consequences of the bug being found?
- Is the equipment to be left in place, if so, for how long? Does it need to be removed, if so what extra risks does this incur. If left in place what is the likelihood of it being discovered and what will be the consequences.
- Is there a safe place to monitor equipment from without leaving vehicles on the road?
- Does the target take any physical or electronic counter measures?
- Can results be gained by OVERT methods? For example, A. If the target is a businessman, can we make a legitimate appointment to meet him and bug the place whilst we are in the building? B. Can we gain access to the building

by posing as a sales rep, telephone engineer, maintenance man or another type of tradesman? If so, you may need some type of disguise and a cover story including false I.D. and a checkable telephone number. C. Can we break into the office or home and use this 'break in' as a cover for planting an electronic device?

- To achieve this, we may need to force a door, a window or a skylight. We will actually need to steal something to cover our tracks; this now leaves us open to the criminal charge of burglary if caught. We may need to carry a jemmy, glasscutter, bolt cutters or a cordless drill. We are now 'going equipped', which could be embarrassing if stopped by the police for a routine matter. We need to work out immediate action drills in case we are disturbed during the breaking and entering (B&E). Consider your actions if caught by 1. the police, 2. a member of the public, 3. the target. Do you, offer resistance, run, or give yourself up. Have you got a cover story ready for each eventuality?

- Let us now consider making a COVERT entry into the target area. We may need to consider some of the following points.

  1. We may need to mount a full-scale physical surveillance operation against the target and or his premises. We will need to note the movements, timings and general routines of the target himself and possibly his family, employees, friends, visiting tradesmen and immediate neighbors. Are the target premises in a good position to carry out this type of in-depth surveillance? Does time permit? Has the target or his immediate neighbors got a dog, CCTV, or other security devices such as proximity lights, which will hamper you at night?

  2. Have you got the knowledge and practical expertise to B&E without leaving evidence of your visit? If not do

you have the necessary contacts to get someone? Will they have the necessary knowledge to plant electronic bugging equipment effectively, or will they have to be escorted thus increasing the risks of being spotted? Do you want them to know what you are up to? Can you trust them, especially if it came to police interrogation? If you do have the capability to B&E yourself you will need, lock picking equipment or a lock pick gun, and gloves etc. You will need to use untraceable bugging equipment. You will also need to destroy all forensic evidence linking you to the scene, such as clothes, footwear etc. You should also have a reliable alibi prepared.

3. You should post lookouts with radios on a secure net using coded signals to provide early warning. These may also be able to act as a diversion to delay the police or any curios neighbors, or even the target returning unexpectedly. In Some circumstances it may be tactically possible to keep the target either occupied during the operation or under surveillance throughout to ensure that he does not return unexpectedly.

4. Once entry to the premises has been gained you should consider the following points: 1. Are any silent alarms or CCTV in operation? 2. Can you be seen from outside? 3. Have you locked the door behind you? 4. Can you photograph documents while you are there, do you need to use flash photography? 5. Use of a Polaroid camera can help to ensure that when you are searching drawers or moving things about, you replace them in the right places. 6. What type of bugs are you going to use, how long will they operate for effectively, remembering that your transmission range will decrease as the batteries run down. Mains powered bugs are usually the best

for long term surveillance so consider placing wall socket bugs in as many rooms as possible. Likewise, a teleinfinity device on the telephone can be accessed from anywhere in the world. You may even consider using a remote video smoke detector camera. If the target takes electronic countermeasures all bugs planted will have to be remotely operated so that they can be switched off during electronic sweeps. These types of bugs are usually only vulnerable to physical searches.

- This type of operation can be fairly risky or because of security measures difficult to mount. Therefore, consider the following alternative methods, A. Can you gain access to the telephone line from outside? B. Can you place a spike mic or wall contact mic anywhere on an outside wall or window? Also, if full electronic surveillance coverage of the target is required remember to bug the grounds or gardens outside. Ensure that all equipment used outside is weather proofed. C. Can you gain access via a garage or shed etc. to an inner wall, or the roof? D. Can a seed mic be used anywhere for example in cracks in the walls, under doors, floors, window frames or gaps in slates around the roof area. E. Is it possible to hire, rent or gain access to the adjoining property to the target premises?

- Even access to the building opposite may offer surveillance possibilities using parabolic or laser mics. If an adjacent room to the target room can be accessed it should be possible to use wall contact mics, fiber optic equipment allowing audio and visual surveillance or possibly seed mics. One method to achieve this would be to gain legitimate access to the target room on the pretext of a meeting, general enquiry etc. Whilst in the target room being interviewed or whatever, we recce the room. We are looking for wall fittings, paintings, pictures, calendars or wall charts etc. We note the exact location of any that are present. At a later date we can drill a small hole very carefully from the adjoining property, through the wall, behind a picture or chart and insert a fiber optic device or seed mic.

- One final point with making a COVERT entry. Under UK law if you B&E without causing any damage and you do not steal anything, then you are only guilty of trespass and not burglary.

ORLANDO "ANDY" WILSON

Orlando has worked internationally at all levels of the specialist security and investigation industry for over 35 years. Over the years, he has become accustomed to the types of complications that can occur, when dealing with international law enforcement agencies and the problem of dealing with kidnapping, organized crime and Mafia groups.

His experience in the international security business began in 1988 when he enlisted in the British army at 17 years of age and volunteered for a 22-month frontline, operational tour in Northern Ireland in an Infantry unit, 4 Platoon, 1 WFR. He then joined his unit's Reconnaissance Platoon, with which he undertook intensive training in small-unit warfare.

Since leaving the British army in 1993, his time spent working in Eastern Europe in the 1990s gave him firsthand experience of the operational procedures of organized criminals and Mafia groups from the former Soviet Union. In addition, he had the opportunity to oversee criminal cases that have been the first of their kind in their respective country. His operations in Mexico training tactical police teams put him in a unique position to understand the war on Narco-Terrorism.

His continuous and ongoing projects focusing on kidnap and ransom prevention in South America, the Caribbean and West Africa have given him the knowledge to formulate practical programs to counter the kidnapping threat.

Orlando is a published author, writer, photographer and has been interviewed by numerous international TV and media outlets on topics ranging from kidnapping, organized crime to maritime piracy. He had his first article published in 1997 in an association magazine and his first book in 2012. He has been interviewed by media outlets ranging from the Professional Mariner Magazine, Newsweek Serbia, Newsweek en Espanol, GrupoMilenio, MundoFox, The New York Times, the BBC, Soldier of Fortune Magazine and others.

Orlando's diverse and continuous operational experience enables him to provide no-nonsense professional services and training programs. His operational investigation and close protection procedures are cutting edge and the most effective commercially available. He is also a founding member and operations manager of Risks Incorporated.

OTHER BOOKS BY ORLANDO

These Books are Available on Amazon!

Non-Fiction Manuals

• Social Navigation: A Practical Survival Guide for Human Interactions

• Counter Insurgency Operations: A tactical Guide for Law Enforcement

• Intelligence Gathering: Front Line HUMINT Considerations

• Caribbean Security Threats: A threat assessment for the islands of the Caribbean

• Gun Range Management: A Guide for Range Managers, Range Safety Officers & Firearms Instructors

• Investigative Journalist Security: Staying Alive to Tell the Truth

• Threat Assessments for Close Protection & Security Management

• Protecting Your Loved Ones: Security Awareness for Parents & Adults

• Close Protection: Luxury & Hostile Environments

• Close Protection & Firearms

• The Close Protection Business

• Home & Office Security: Protection of Residencies & Businesses

• Travel Security: Personal Travel & Vehicle Security

• Counter Terrorism: Terrorist Attack Response

• Kidnap & Ransom: The Essentials of Kidnapping Prevention

• Shoot First & Shoot Last: The Real-World Guide to Pistol Craft

Crime Fiction

- The Shoot: An Assassin's World
- Vengeance: The Art of Pain
- The Collectors: Death is Easy, Life is Hard
- Reglas Mexicanas: A Life Without Pain, Is Not A Life

Photo Books

- Athens Lockdown 2020 in Pictures
- Wandering in Serbia
- Vigilantes of Imo – Nigerian Vigilante Life in Pictures